Tell Me Why

Wynonna

MW00856696

ISBN 0-7935-2697-3

Hal Leonard Publishing Corporation
7777 West Bluemound Road P.O. Box 13819 Milwaukee, WI 53213

FATHER SUN

Words and Music by SHERYL CROW
and JAY OLIVER

Please don't for - get __ me, Fa - ther Sun, __ Fa - ther Sun. __

I think I hear him whis - per - ing, _

L.H.

GIRLS WITH GUITARS

Words and Music by
MARY-CHAPIN CARPENTER

turned fif - teen with great ___ ex - pec - ta - tions. Her
Sat - ur - day nights she fol - lowed her bro - ther. It was
old Chev - y van just sit - tin' in the drive - way,

old - er bro - ther knew some - thin' was up. He
socks and stock - in's on the old gym floor. While
filled to the gills with all ___ of her stuff. She cut a

D.S. al Co

Now there's an

Gives a lit - tle grin and blows_____ a - way the

I JUST DROVE BY

Words and Music by
KIMMIE RHODES

Moderate country ballad

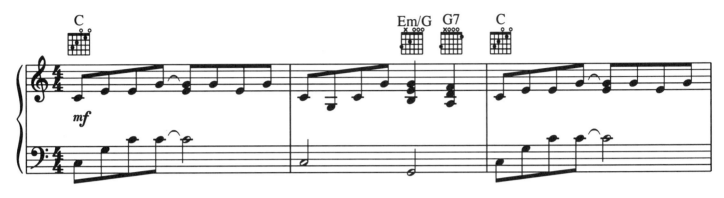

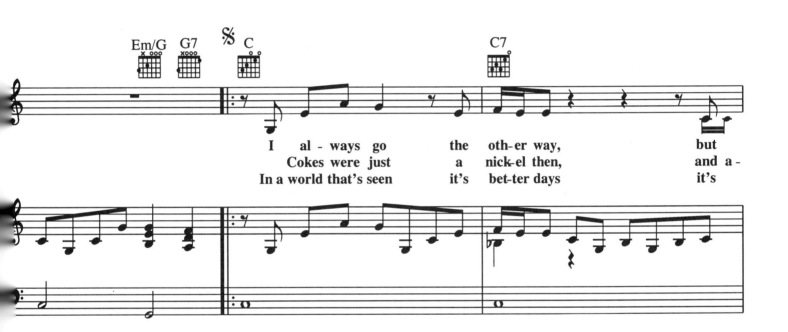

I al-ways go the oth-er way, but
Cokes were just a nick-el then, and a-
In a world that's seen it's bet-ter days it's

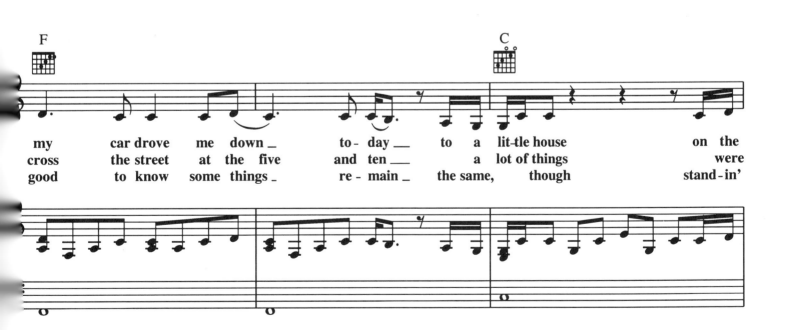

my car drove me down to-day to a lit-tle house on the
cross the street at the five and ten a lot of things were
good to know some things re-main the same, though stand-in'

just drove by to see _____ if things had changed.

IS IT OVER YET

Words and Music by
BILLY KIRSCH

Tell me when   I can o - pen my eyes. ___
A tax - i's wait - ing   in the drive - way for you. ___

JUST LIKE NEW

Words and Music by
JESSE WINCHESTER

Moderate country rock

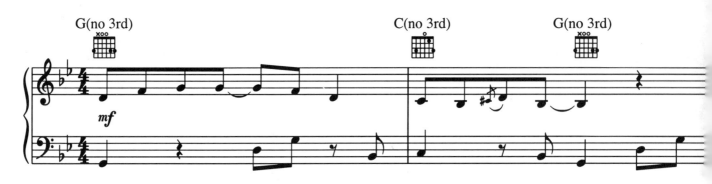

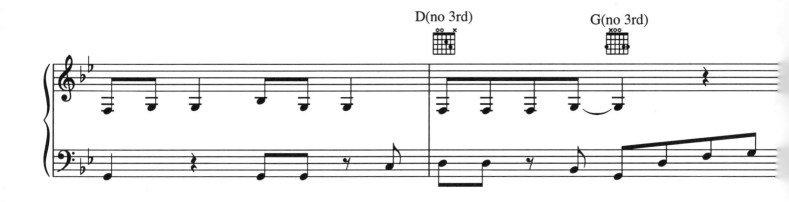

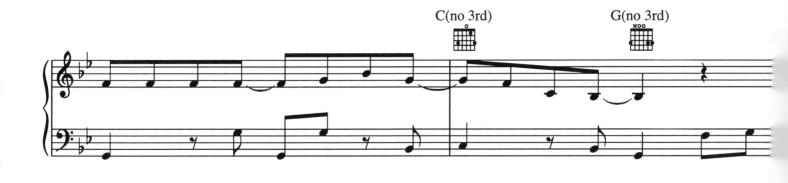

29

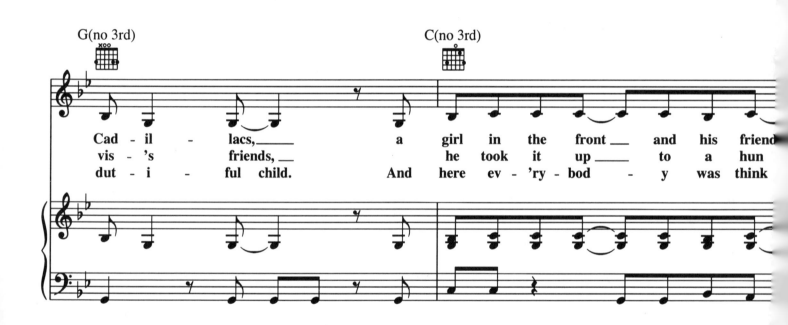

LET'S MAKE A BABY KING

Words and Music by
JESSE WINCHESTER

Bright country rock

Once up-on a Christ-mas morn-in' there was a
you re-mem-ber lit-tle King Dav-id;
Instrumental
we could use a rev-o-lu-tion; the

pret-ty lit-tle ba-by boy. _____ It seems_
he's the lit-tle ba-by's kin. _____ He's
world is turned up-side down. _____ And

___ like I re-mem-ber sad - ness
cous - in to a man named John, _____ and I
we need a new di - rec - tion; we've got to

ming-l-in' in ___ the joy. ___ For
know you all re-mem-ber him. ___ And
turn this whole thing a - round. __ And

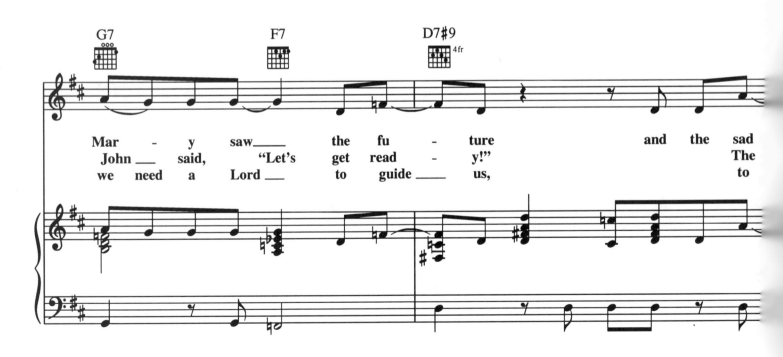

G7   F7   D7#9   4fr

Mar - y saw ___ the fu - ture and the sad
John ___ said, "Let's get read - y!" The
we need a Lord ___ to guide ___ us, to

ONLY LOVE

Words and Music by MARCUS HUMMON
and ROGER MURRAH

40

ROCK BOTTOM

Words and Music by BUDDY BUIE
and J.R. COBB

Lyrics:

When you hit rock bot - tom, you've got
law of the jung - le is got the

two ways to go: straight up and side -
law of the land, good luck stay - in' a -

44

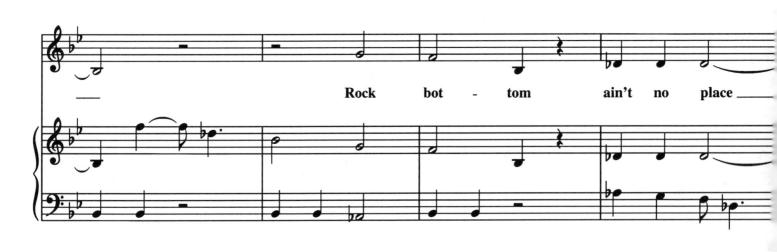

Rock bot - tom ain't no place

To Coda

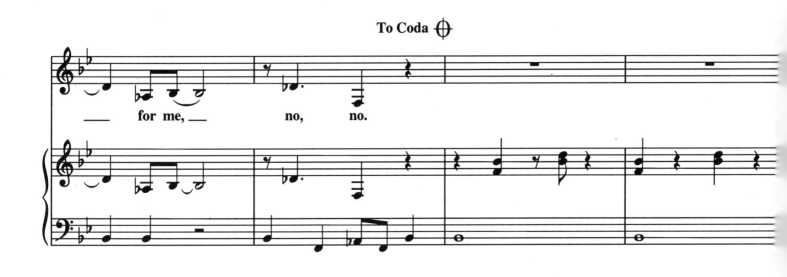

for me, __ no, no.

No, __ no. __

TELL ME WHY

Words and Music by
KARLA BONOF

Ev - 'ry-where I look the
Ev - 'ry-where I go you're

sun is shin - ing,
in my shad - ow;

but it's al - ways rain - ing here ___ in - side. ___
when I turn a - round, there's no ___ one there. ___

THAT WAS YESTERDAY

Words and Music by
NAOMI JUD[...]

But that was yes - ter - day,_ *yeah, honey,* that was yes - ter - day.____

And so it